DEADLY DISEASES

Typhoid FEVER
A Deadly Infection

Percy Leed

Lerner Publications ◆ Minneapolis

Copyright © 2022 by Lerner Publishing Group, Inc.

All rights reserved. International copyright secured. No part of this book may be reproduced, stored in a retrieval system, or transmitted in any form or by any means—electronic, mechanical, photocopying, recording, or otherwise—without the prior written permission of Lerner Publishing Group, Inc., except for the inclusion of brief quotations in an acknowledged review.

Lerner Publications Company
An imprint of Lerner Publishing Group, Inc.
241 First Avenue North
Minneapolis, MN 55401 USA

For reading levels and more information, look up this title at www.lernerbooks.com.

Main body text set in ITC Franklin Gothic Std.
Typeface provided by Adobe Systems.

Designer: Mary Ross

Library of Congress Cataloging-in-Publication Data

Names: Leed, Percy, 1968– author.
Title: Typhoid fever : a deadly infection / Percy Leed.
Description: Minneapolis : Lerner Publications, [2022] | Series: Deadly diseases (updog books) | Includes bibliographical references and index. | Audience: Ages 8–11 | Audience: Grades 4–6 | Summary: "Each year typhoid fever affects up to 20 million people. Readers will uncover how scientists are fighting back with clean water and vaccination"— Provided by publisher.
Identifiers: LCCN 2020043284 (print) | LCCN 2020043285 (ebook) | ISBN 9781728428383 (library binding) | ISBN 9781728431277 (paperback) | ISBN 9781728430652 (ebook)
Subjects: LCSH: Typhoid fever—Juvenile literature.
Classification: LCC RC187 .L44 2022 (print) | LCC RC187 (ebook) | DDC 616.9/272—dc23

LC record available at https://lccn.loc.gov/2020043284
LC ebook record available at https://lccn.loc.gov/2020043285

Manufactured in the United States of America
1-49375-49479-1/12/2021

Table of Contents

Typhoid fever

A man rushes to the ER. He has a fever. His head and belly hurt.

He has typhoid fever. It affects
millions each year.

Typhoid is caused by bacteria.

bacteria: tiny living things that can make you sick

A person with typhoid has head and stomach pain. The patient's temperature may reach 104°F (40°C).

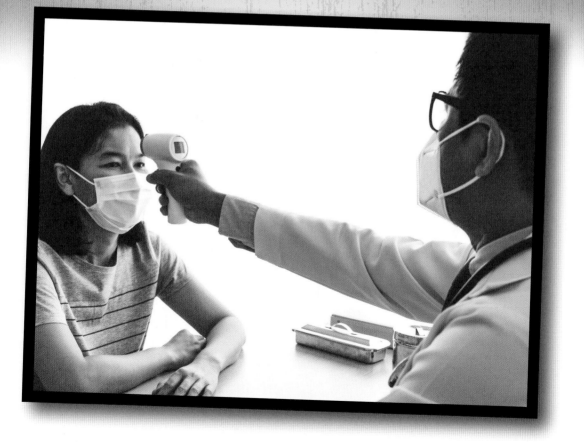

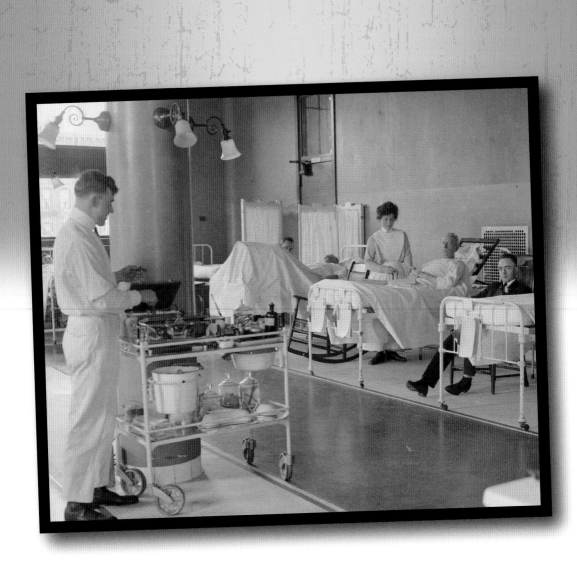

In the early 1900s, the US had a lot of typhoid cases. Now typhoid is rare in the US.

It's most common in South Asia.

UP NEXT!
Typhoid Today.

Progress

Scientists have been working to stop typhoid.

It often spreads through contaminated water.

contaminated: dirty or polluted

UP CLOSE

The image on the right shows
the germ that causes typhoid.

Water treatment helps stop contamination.
Many countries use water treatment systems.

Around 1900, doctors made a typhoid vaccine. It slowed the spread of the illness.

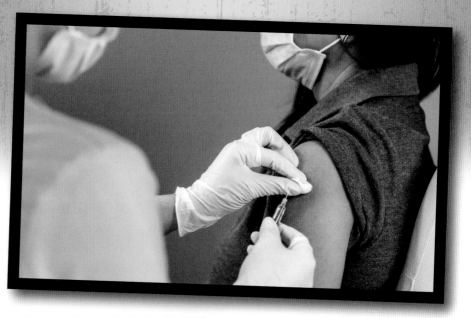

vaccine: a treatment that protects against sickness

UP NEXT!
Staying Safe.

Prevention

Healthy habits can help prevent typhoid and other illnesses.

Washing your hands gets rid of bad bacteria.

Heat kills germs. Eat well-cooked foods.

Before visiting places with typhoid, get the vaccine. Drink bottled water there.

Follow healthy habits to keep your body strong and healthy.

DOCTOR YOU!

Which patient do you think has typhoid?

Patient A
fever
headache
sore throat

Patient B
fever
headache
bellyache

Answer: Patient B

Glossary

bacteria: tiny living things that can make you sick

contaminated: dirty or polluted

vaccine: a treatment that protects against sickness

Check It Out!

Alkire, Jessie. *Super Gross Germ Projects*. Minneapolis: Abdo, 2019.

Being Safe in the Kitchen
https://kidshealth.org/en/kids/safe-in-kitchen.html?WT
.ac=ctg#cathouse

Leed, Percy. *Guts (A Stomach-Turning Augmented Reality Experience)*. Minneapolis: Lerner Publications, 2021.

Mould, Steve. *The Bacteria Book*. New York: DK, 2018.

Typhoid Fever
https://kids.britannica.com/kids/article/typhoid-fever
/435835

What Are Germs?
https://kidshealth.org/en/kids/germs.html

Index

Photo Acknowledgments

Image credits: Drazen Zigic/Shutterstock.com, p. 4; Aleksandr Ozerov/ Shutterstock.com, p. 5; as-artmedia/Shutterstock.com, p. 6; plo/ Shutterstock.com, p. 7; Library of Congress (LC-DIG-ggbain-24337), p. 8; Serg!o/Wikimedia Commons (CC BY-SA 3.0), p. 9; Infot/ Shutterstock.com, p. 10; NinaMalyna/Shutterstock.com, p. 11; decade3d - anatomy online/Shutterstock.com, p. 13; Florida Water Daily/flickr (CC BY 2.0), p. 14; BaLL LunLa/Shutterstock.com, p. 15; Monkey Business Images/Shutterstock.com, p. 16; Daisy Daisy/ Shutterstock.com, pp. 17, 20; moreimages/Shutterstock.com, p. 18; Darren Baker/Shutterstock.com, p. 19.

Cover: decade3d - anatomy online/Shutterstock.com.